C000141508

Profit
Improvement
in a week

TIM LEVEY

Hodder & Stoughton

A MEMBER OF THE HODDER HEADLINE GROUP

Orders: please contact Bookpoint Ltd, 130 Milton Park, Abingdon, Oxon
OX14 4SB.
Telephone: (44) 01235 827720, Fax: (44) 01235 400454. Lines are open from
9.00–6.00, Monday to Saturday, with a 24 hour message answering service.
You can also order through our website www.madaboutbooks.com

British Library Cataloguing in Publication Data
A catalogue record for this title is available from The British Library

ISBN 0 340 81692 9

First published	2004
Impression number	10 9 8 7 6 5 4 3 2 1
Year	2008 2007 2006 2005 2004

Typeset by SX Composing DTP, Rayleigh, Essex.
Printed in Great Britain for Hodder & Stoughton Educational, a division of
Hodder Headline, 338 Euston Road, London NW1 3BH, by
Cox & Wyman Ltd, Reading, Berkshire.

Papers used in this book are natural, renewable and recyclable products. They
are made from wood grown in sustainable forests. The logging and
manufacturing processess conform to the environmental regulations of the
country of origin.

■■■■■ C O N T E N T S ■■■■■

Acknowledgements

The author and publishers would especially like to thank the
following organisations and people for the use of illustrations
and information in this publication:

- James Cross and the partners of Reeves & Neylan
- Barry R. Schimel, C.P.A. and Gary Kravitz – Authors of *All
  About Earnings* (Capital Books Inc. Virginia USA)

■ I N T R O D U C T I O N ■

In reality it's quite easy to improve the profits of any business, and see some positive effects on the profit line in under a week as well! Just go ahead and cut costs anywhere you like on Monday morning, and by Friday afternoon you can probably point to higher profits.

But what about next week and the week after that? Randomly cutting costs can only be a short-term approach in desperate circumstances. If that were the way to maximise profits over the long term, then every business would do it. Experience suggests that businesses that do take this approach tend not to be around for very long. Our goal in a week is to go beyond random cost cutting and outline an approach to improving profitability over the long term.

Many businesses work hard to improve their profitability. In general, however, this will be through a disjointed collection of different projects, which have probably been formulated in reaction to an urgent need or crisis. This book will explain how it is better to have some system that identifies and deals with issues before the need becomes urgent.

One new groundbreaking idea makes it possible to substantially improve the profits of a business. Unfortunately such ideas are few and far between. As an alternative to spending time looking for something that might not exist, all businesses could instead improve profits by turning their attention to a number of smaller areas in their operations.

This Profit Improvement process has three key phases:

1 Information Gathering
2 Idea Generation
3 Implementation Guidance

The week ahead

Sunday: We will define what is meant by Profit Improvement and explain why this process is more effective than just providing a list of general areas to look at.

Monday: We will consider the importance of incentives in the process, and suggest some alternatives to consider in preparation for different stages throughout the coming week.

Tuesday: The Information Gathering work starts by checking and reviewing the current direction of the business (its Intention).

Wednesday: Analysing the business from a number of different perspectives will complete the Information Gathering. This will entail looking generally at the business and then going into more detail on issues that this identifies. The result will be a list of the key issues facing the business.

Thursday: The key issues for which there are no immediate solutions are now presented to the staff in a workshop setting. Their ideas for solutions are generated, discussed and captured in an Ideas Plan.

Friday: For the project to be successful, the ideas agreed so far now need to be implemented as effectively and efficiently as possible. Today we will look at a structured approach to implementation that reduces the chance of costly failure.

Saturday: With the ideas now agreed, the improvement in those areas needs to be inspected and monitored if the momentum is to be kept going into the coming weeks and months.

Introduction to Profit Improvement

Today we will look at what 'profit' is. We will then look at three standard types of businesses and consider examples of how such businesses do not maximise the profit that they make. We will also consider the main reasons why suggestion schemes, which are a common tool in profit improvement, fail and therefore what needs to be in place for such an initiative to be successful.

It would be naïve to suggest that businesses exist solely to make profits. People want more than that. However, businesses cannot exist for long without making profits and generating money. This profit, or self-generated income, provides resources for expansion and reward for the risk that shareholders take on. You can live off previously generated profits or borrow in the short term, but long term you must somehow make a profit to remain viable.

To understand that there is more to Profit Improvement than cost cutting we need to start by defining what 'profit' is. The *Oxford English Dictionary* presents a technical definition as 'the excess of returns over outlay'. Immediately, therefore, we have 'increasing the returns' as an alternative to 'reducing the outlay'.

Retail and wholesale businesses
Such businesses have been in existence since the original days of bartering and are alive and well in any street market. You buy goods from one party (the outlay) and sell the same goods to a number of others (the returns). So long as you

have sold the goods for more money than you paid, then you have made a profit.

Such businesses may try to maximise their profits by cutting their costs or getting as many customers as possible, but such tactics ignore two other ways of improving profitability:

- Increasing the value of each sale – by encouraging each customer to buy something else
- Increasing the frequency of sales – by encouraging each customer to return soon!

These two alternatives recognise that it is easier to sell to an existing customer than it is to find, and then sell to, a new customer.

Manufacturing businesses
In terms of a typical manufacturing business, its 'returns' will be the sales income that comes from despatching its products to customers. Its 'outlay' will come under two general headings of:

- Direct outlays in manufacturing the products, such as raw materials, labour costs and factory costs (light, heat, etc.)
- Other costs not directly related to the manufacturing, such as sales and marketing costs, administrative costs and finance costs

Suppose, however, that the business that you were in had low customer retention for your industry at 60 per cent. You find that 5 per cent of goods delivered are rejected and returned and that staff retention is also low at 50 per cent. The accounts of the business may show that it is making a small profit, but investors require a greater return. While cost cutting can quickly reduce the outlays, it is often the case that the cuts will be made in areas that can make the results worse in the longer term. For example, cutting the sales and marketing budget probably leads to an even lower sales income, and cutting production staff could increase the percentage of goods rejected by customers.

The root causes of the lost profits tend to be things such as:

- Materials being badly stored, so that purchase orders are made for items held in stock
- Unclear order instructions from the sales staff to the production staff
- Bottlenecks in the production process that are left unaddressed

These and many similar problems get lost in bigger numbers. It is difficult to see that sales income is lower than it could be, or that material and labour costs are higher than they could be. Then there is a knock on effect in that other costs such as sales and marketing costs may be higher than they need to be to make up for the poor customer retention. Even worse, staff morale never improves as the profits are never high enough to generate the cash to re-invest in training or new equipment.

Service businesses
These businesses will be faced with a different set of issues from the manufacturing business, but the result will be the

same. At the beginning there is a marketing process to make potential clients aware of the services on offer. At the end, money is banked and a follow-up contract sought. Between these two there are many things that can get in the way to suppress profits. Often the job is not completed as fast as it could be, or is sometimes not even completed at all. Because productive staff tend to be by far the greatest cost, the main drains of profitability will be those that affect them.

These typically include:

* Inadequate planning of a job so that it is not completed as efficiently as possible
* A poor induction procedure for new employees, which means that it takes longer for them to generate profits
* Work being done by too high a grade of staff (under-delegation)
* Negative attitudes in the staff team which go unaddressed

While the main profit problems in a manufacturing business get hidden in the 'cost of sales' line, in a service business they are more likely to be found in the 'staff costs' line.

The problem

Just from looking at these three different types of businesses, it can be seen that there are many reasons why profits are not maximised. With every business being unique, the degree to which each possible issue is a factor will differ. So with that background, how can there exist a single approach to Profit Improvement that can apply to all businesses?

The solution

For a long-term solution to Profit Improvement an approach is needed that recognises that every business is different, if it is to identify efficiently where the returns could be higher and the outlay lower. Just as the profitability of a business is determined by how well it performs a myriad of small tasks, so the profit can be improved effectively and ethically by addressing these many tasks. You could bring in an external consultant to find the solutions for you, but usually the answers are *inside* the business already.

This answer is clear when you go behind the technical definition of profit and recognise that the 'returns' and 'outlay' do not belong to separate worlds, but are interlinked. Profits (or losses) are the result of the levels of commitment, creativity, discipline, effort and energy of the *people* in the business. These people are often the biggest outlay of a business, but they also control most of the other outlays and have decisive influence over revenues and returns, if only by the level of customer care that they provide. With profits therefore being the result of human endeavour, any Profit Improvement initiatives need to capture the ideas of those people who help to create it.

Who should be involved?

In attempting to improve the profits of a business, one problem is that too many people believe that only they know the solutions. Senior management, for example, often maintain that it is 'their responsibility' to improve the profits and are unwilling to share this. In the meantime, everyone down to the most junior person in a business believes that they know how to make improvements. Even the advisers of the business, be they the accountant or the bank manager, believe that they have something to contribute.

The secret of successful Profit Improvement is to use *everyone's* ideas and abilities to the greatest advantage. As many people as possible need to be able to contribute. The best ideas can then be agreed by consensus and swiftly put into practice. This needs to be done in a planned way, as the haphazard approach that most businesses take means that it will take longer to achieve an imperfect result.

Why do suggestion schemes fail?

Many businesses have tried and failed to seek ideas for improvement by getting all the staff together and asking them for their ideas. Others have avoided this direct approach by running a suggestion scheme. These tend to be started in a blaze of intensity but can quickly fizzle out.

The reasons for these failed attempts include:

- Staff are not prepared for the request for ideas
- Rewards to the staff for contributing ideas are non-existent or unclear
- The ideas are not recognised and valued by management
- There is no structured follow-up with staff after an idea has been put forward
- Often the best ideas do not get put into practice

Any one of these could be enough to make the whole initiative fail, so the process needs to be robust enough to cover all of these issues.

The benefits and features of this process

The process that will be followed has the benefit of ensuring that the many ideas generated that will improve profitability are implemented as efficiently as possible. The features are that:

Before ideas are sought:

- Management is agreed upon the general direction of the business. This enables them to give a message to staff that focuses their efforts.
- A scheme that incentivises Profit Improvement is agreed, so that there is something in it for everyone who takes part. This will make the seeking and collecting of ideas easier, but more importantly the scheme should extend to the implementation of those ideas as well.

As ideas are sought:

- Many people in the business become involved, which means that teamwork is improved and more progress is made faster, particularly in implementing ideas.
- The ideas focus on the issues of your particular business, which is unique. This means that you do not get side-tracked looking for issues that may be common in other businesses or sectors, but not in your own.
- The ideas come from inside the business, which means that they have more chance of being adopted.

After the ideas have been collected:

- Responsibility for each idea is taken by one individual, who will not necessarily be from the management group.
- Each idea is supported by an estimate of the increase in profitability that will result.
- The overall plan is prioritised, so that resources can be directed at the most important issues.
- The implementation of projects is rigorously followed up, so that adjustments can be made if necessary.

Prerequisite for success

Of great importance to the success of a major Profit Improvement exercise is the mindset of the senior management of the business. At the very least, they all need to have the intention of doing something positive. If they are truly unhappy about the present situation, even irritated and impatient for improvement, then so much the better. On the other hand, if management is feeling comfortable with performance and profits, then this process is unlikely to be of interest to them at the moment.

So are you motivated enough to want to improve profitability? You can find out by answering the question, 'What would higher profits enable me to do?' The answers could be more salary or dividends, more funds to help you in retirement, the reduction or removal of debt finance, the ability to invest more in the business, or maybe to maximise the value of the business prior to it being sold. There must be compelling reasons for going ahead because, as with many processes, Profit Improvement means change, and change is difficult.

> 'Profit Improvement is the result of implementing ideas in a structured way.'

This phrase sums up the key to success in the process!

A general test of your resolve before proceeding is to answer the following questions.

	1 = I strongly disagree 4 = I have no strong feelings 7 = I strongly agree						
	1	2	3	4	5	6	7
I am unhappy with the current profitability of the business							
I am prepared to do something positive about the problems that we face							
I do not think that staff are working together as a team							
I believe that there are opportunities that pass us by							
I find that once we decide to do something, it gets done							
I know that business could be done more efficiently							
I agree that the answers to improving profits are in the business somewhere							

If you score in the top half, that is above 28, then you clearly have a positive attitude towards this process and would benefit greatly from following it through the week. The higher your score, the more certain this is.

Before you get too far . . .

Part of the process is to generate ideas and implement them, but if the business is working on too many other initiatives already, then you could only add to the problem. Many businesses have 'initiative indigestion', with very little ever getting done.

The first thing to do, before you get too far into the week, is to try to bring to completion, or at least clear from your desk, projects that are being worked on at the moment.

Make a list of all the initiatives that the business is working on and assess them in terms of the following:

- How complete are they? Estimate this as a percentage to give you an idea of how much work remains.
- Who is working on each one? Identify the person who is responsible.
- How important is each initiative? Grade these on a scale of 1 to 5, with 1 being vitally important and 5 being a waste of time.
- How much input is needed? Again on a scale of 1 to 5, with 1 being very little and 5 being massive.
- How much will the completion of the initiative increase the profits of the business?

Now spend some time assessing these initiatives. Divide them into the initiatives that you are working on and ones that others in the business are working on. Should any of them be stopped because they are unworkable, or are past their useful date, or will not contribute to the performance and profitability of the business?

If the person responsible for doing many of these jobs turns out to be you, then question whether you are the right person. Could someone else be rewarded for taking projects on, so freeing up your own time?

Spend time now getting the worthwhile ones completed or at least on track. There is no need to clear all of the projects; otherwise you may never get started! Having done this you will be ready and prepared for the week ahead!

Final preparations for the week

With these things taken care of, it is now time to put the
plans in place for the week. The most important of these is to
consider how you will let everyone in the business know that
this week is going to be a 'Profit Improvement Week' for the
business. Staff will be able to contribute more effectively if
they are aware what will be happening each day and where
their help may be needed. An announcement that there will
be rewards for helping the business should also go down
well.

Incentive schemes

Today an important foundation needs to be put in place before the detailed work can start.

The owner or the manager who wants to start this Profit Improvement process has probably got a strong motivation of some sort. They will have decided, or at least hope, that the rewards for pursuing this process will be worth the time and cost involved. That will be enough if they plan to do all of the work themselves, but if they want to involve other people from the business in the exercise, then there is a need to think about how it is planned to incentivise them.

Consideration needs to be given to rewards at each level of the process therefore:

- People need to open up about what is happening at the moment
- You need to encourage them to come up with ideas
- They then need to be encouraged to implement the best ideas

Now your people should be encouraged that it is to their long-term advantage to make the organisation more profitable. It can be tempting to think that there is therefore no need to incentivise staff and that they will be sufficiently motivated to assist. Human beings in general have a need for recognition and reward, especially for special efforts, which is what this process will demand in the implementation stage.

If you already have a bonus scheme for staff that is related to the profitability of the business, then you have a head start. Staff should already be aware that they would be rewarded as a team should the business be more profitable. Letting them know that there will be an opportunity this week to add to that bonus will get you a long way. All that you may need in addition is some individual incentives to complement this.

Possible incentives

The most obvious incentive is cash, but there are plenty of other options to consider:

Gift certificates
These could be particularly useful in rewarding individual ideas or contributions. If they are being used for larger rewards then ask the recipient to tell everyone what they spent the certificate on.

Donations to charity
You may have a charity that the entire business supports, or you may want to let each employee donate his or her reward.

Paid time off

The incentives do not need to be financial. With modern-day living meaning that spare time is at a premium, paid time off could be valued more than money. It does, however, need to be made clear that this will be a one-off reward rather than a permanent entitlement.

Dinner out

This could be as individuals or as a group. You may want to do this anyway, in addition to any other rewards, to make sure the whole team gets something out of contributing.

Travel or holiday vouchers

These would be good for the larger reward of implementing an idea, but not for smaller rewards.

Health club membership

Again, this could be for individuals or for a group. It may be something that is worth doing anyway given the likely reduction in rates of absenteeism that result from staff being both physically and mentally healthier.

Entertainment tickets

A good idea, but they need to be handled with care. Will the entertainment that you choose be suitable for everyone? Different generations have different concepts of 'entertainment'.

Choosing the incentives

Not all incentive schemes work! A badly designed or implemented scheme can do more damage than good. The guidelines of a successful scheme are that it must be:

- Easy to install and operate
- Easily understood and perceived as fair by everyone
- Linked to the results required
- Given now rather than later

There is one other important factor to consider. There is nothing worse than spending a great deal of time and resources designing an incentive scheme to support the programme, only to find that people are not interested in the incentive and therefore are not minded to contribute. The only failsafe way to ensure that the rewards will have the required effect is to ask your team what they want.

This is the ideal opportunity, at the beginning of the working week, to introduce the Profit Improvement initiative to the business. Communicate to them an outline of what is planned for the week, how you would like them to contribute and ask them what incentives would they like to choose. They can either be presented with a list similar to the above, or throw things open and give them a blank piece of paper. The team could surprise you by asking for something that you might never have thought of, but if they tell you it will really motivate them.

After the team have told you what incentives they value most, involve them in the design, development and implementation of the scheme. It has more credibility if they have had a hand in creating it. That way the result should be one that they understand, and this will be a great advantage later in the week.

How much should the incentives be?

For each phase of the process there will need to be a different incentive scheme. You may not think it necessary to incentivise the Information Gathering stage – normally people are only too willing to have their say about what is happening at the moment, and this may be the one phase when incentives are least required. During the Idea Generation phase, it is best to have several small incentives in place, as these tend to be better than a few large ones. The unusual coins or notes in the currency are best; otherwise small gift certificates are good to hand out.

When you reach the Implementation phase, it might be tempting to just go for a percentage of savings achieved. However, you may want to put a maximum limit on the sum payable for each idea, or offer a scale of fixed sums depending upon the improvement achieved. The advantage of agreeing on a fixed sum is that it limits the amount of discussion that is required about the size of the gain.

General rules on incentives

Don't reward activities.
Do reward results.

Don't tamper with basic pay rates; keep them at competitive market levels.
Do use incentives to take pay to the higher end of the market.

Don't make promises that you cannot afford to keep.
Do fund incentive schemes from the additional funds that they generate.

Don't rely on individual incentives alone.
Do incentivise teams.

Don't make the scheme too complicated.
Do involve staff in the design of the scheme.

Final words on incentives

Be aware that the whole area of incentives is a minefield when it comes to taxation. As a general rule, gifts provided to an employee by reason of that employment are taxable and the tax authorities take a special interest in these arrangements.

Secondly, if you are doing this more than once then you will need to re-think the incentives each time. After a while any reward can lose its motivational power. It can get to seem like an entitlement and people will come to rely on it as part of pay.

CASH REWARD CEREMONY

Finally, now that the structure of incentives has been agreed, this should be published so that everyone in the business is clear about them.

Intentions review

Today you will start the work involved in gathering information in order to work out where the business is at the moment and, more importantly, where it should be heading. This has been termed its 'Intention'.

Today's objective is to review, test and if necessary revise the current Intention of the business. If possible, this should be done in a group with other key members of management.

Step 1 – your present Intention

To start, write down where you believe the business is heading in the long term. This will be *the present Intention of the business*.

This is a concept similar to a 'mission' or 'vision'. However, as will be seen, its definition is more specific than either of these. Missions and visions, which tend to be condensed into a written statement, can be the result of many different

processes. At one extreme they come in a blinding flash of inspiration to the business owner or Managing Director, and they are presented to staff almost as a message from above.

At the other extreme, missions and visions can be the result of a lengthy period of analysis about where the business is at the moment and where it should be heading. Businesses can be examined from every conceivable angle to ensure that nothing is missed out and the exercise will cover both internal and external issues. Sometimes this analysis can go on over many months.

The problem with this latter approach is that *you* have just one day in which to get your direction formulated and agreed. What is needed is a quick strategy review that does not run the risk of getting stuck in the detail or paralysed by analysis.

The Intention of a business is defined as *the overall aim of the business, which demonstrates specifically how the business will meet the needs of its customers in the context of the marketplace*. This highlights two fundamental parts of the question, 'Where is the business now?':

- The business environment and climate
- The needs of the customers or clients

If you think that this is too easy and simplistic, then consider successful and profitable businesses that you know. In all cases you should find that, whether by luck or judgement, they do indeed provide a product or service that customers or clients want in sufficient volume for them to be successful or profitable. The marketplace that they are operating in will be conducive to their success, or at least does not hinder it. Now think about some unsuccessful businesses that you know, or ones that were successful and then lost their way. See if one of these two parts is missing. If you believe that both parts are or were there when it was unsuccessful, then the only alternative is that the business struggled as a result of the internal operations of the business. We have the rest of the week in which to address internal issues. But first things first . . .

If correctly constructed, the 'Intention' will be valuable later in the week, as it should:

- Make clear to staff just where the business is heading and how their efforts can help.
- Assist with the selection of the issues that need to be tackled for the business to achieve its Intention.
- Assist teams with prioritising the Profit Improvement ideas that come from the process.

So how was the Intention that you recorded as the first exercise?

Intention credibility test
Is the Intention customer or client orientated?

Is it still relevant in the current marketplace?

In the light of the above definition, are you still happy with it?

If you believe that your written Intention honestly passes the credibility test, then the rest of the day is yours. Take a rest and prepare for Wednesday!

If what you have written was formulated some time ago, or does not otherwise pass the credibility test, then it is likely to be in need of a reassessment.

Step 2 – business environment and climate

Being inside a business can be likened to a ride in a raft through white water. Miss the current and you are left paddling hard but going nowhere. Choose to ride where the current is dangerously strong and you risk plummeting down, out of control and heading for possible destruction.

But getting the strength of current and the route right, you find that everyone can work together to get through the white water in the fastest time and with the best results. Throughout the journey the occupants feel exhilarated.

So this part of the review is about testing the currents. This will be tackled in two parts:

- Porter's Five Forces model, which considers the various types of competitive forces of which a business needs to be aware
- Other key external factors that are likely to be outside the control of the business, but shape the business environment in ways that cannot be ignored

The following questions should be answered as honestly as possible, giving as much detail as possible.

Porter's Five Forces

1 *Competition within the industry*: Rivalry between competitors can take many forms beyond price competition. Businesses can focus on after-sales service, product quality and even safety. This competition tends to be more aggressive if the industry is not growing, has high fixed costs, is fragmented or sometimes when there are high growth rates that are attracting new competitors.

So who are your key competitors at the moment? Where are they based or is this irrelevant? Which markets are they focusing on and what appears to be their strategy?

2 *Customers*: Customers are more powerful when they are large relative to your business or when the purchases represent a high proportion of their costs, as this improves their ability and need to bargain.

How much of this is relevant to your business? Would any of your customers be interested in integrating backwards and buying either you or one of your competitors? What could be the impact of that happening?

3 *Suppliers*: Relative size is also a source of power here. Suppliers are powerful when there are only a few of them serving an industry and there are few substitutes. They can then raise prices, reduce quality or tighten credit terms at will.

Does this apply to you? Would any of your suppliers be interested in integrating forwards and buying you or your competitors? What would be the impact of that?

4 *Other potential entrants to the market*: New entrants mean
   more capacity, which usually increases competition.
   Where barriers to entry are low, competition can become
   fierce, with competitors regularly entering the market.

   Who might those entrants be? How likely is their
   intervention and how would they make it work? Could
   you increase the barriers to entry to protect yourself and
   put off potential entrants?

5 *Substitute products or services*: Substitutes are alternative
   products that perform in a similar manner to your own
   products or services. They tend to be produced in markets
   that make high profits and will be marketed more
   aggressively. As we become more innovative, no product
   or service can consider itself immune to the threat of
   substitution.

   What substitute products and services are there that
   could affect your own market? What could be the impact
   of this?

Other key external factors
The other factors to take into account can be covered using
the acronym STEEPLE, which stands for Sociological,
Technological, Economic, Environmental, Political, Legal and
Ethical. Many of these are interrelated. For example, changes
in demographics can lead to political initiatives to regulate
the economy which result in new laws.

If a business does not or is unable to respond to serious
pressures from around it, then survival can be threatened.
Changed buying patterns, new legislation and especially the
general state of the economy can alter the rules of the game.

So now consider the following:

Sociological: What are the key sociological and demographic forces that shape your business? These could include people's attitude to 'profit' and attitudes to work. How do these affect you and is there a predictable trend? This could include the impact of an ageing population, a trend of businesses to cut commuting time by allowing their staff to work from home, or a movement towards more part-time and self-employed workers.

Technological: What are the key technological forces that shape your business? Few companies are immune from considering this. How do these advances affect you? This could include the increased speed and reducing cost of computing power and the internet.

Economic: What are the key economic forces that shape your business, both domestically and internationally? How do these affect your business? The economy can be viewed on a scale from booming to recessionary and each will have different connotations for business. Levels of inflation and interest rates can also have an effect.

Environmental: What are the areas that governments and people are becoming more aware and concerned about? These could be pollution, waste or health issues. How do these impact the costs of doing business?

Political: What are the key political forces that shape your business? How do these affect you? These might be the increasing complexity of labour laws and other areas of increased regulation such as Health and Safety. Is more competition being encouraged?

Legal: Some sectors are more heavily regulated than others. What are the legal forces at work and what could be changing?

Ethical: What ethical issues appear to be important at the moment? These could include a greater willingness for people to sue or decisions to boycott businesses whose ethics are questionable.

Any business that is too inward looking is liable to stagnate. What has the above analysis revealed about the business environment and climate that affects you?

Step 3 – customer or client analysis

The second aspect to consider in choosing a business's Intention is the needs of its customers or clients. History is littered with products that looked interesting, but which too few people wanted or needed and therefore did not buy.

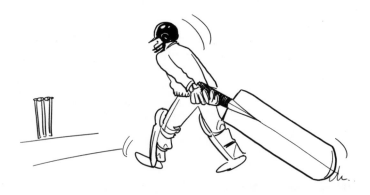

This section will seek to identify who your most important customers are and establish what they need that you either provide or do not provide at the moment.

1 Group your customers into broad categories. Identify the top 20 per cent who provide the greatest contribution to profits. These are not necessarily your largest customers, particularly where they can exert buying power over you.

2 What factors affect the purchasing decisions of each group? This could be quality, service, a key relationship or price. Why do these people buy from you and why might they go to your competitors?

3 What feedback have you or your frontline staff had from your customers? What do they value and what needs to be improved?

4 What do your key customers ask you for that you do not provide at the moment?

5 Is there anything that your key customers are likely to ask you for, if only they knew that you could provide it or that they needed it?

It may be that you cannot answer all of these questions as fully as you would like. Possibly the feedback that your staff receive does not get back to you. If so, this will be something that you will want to bear in mind for later in the week. For now, asking some members of staff for information will give you some clues.

Step 4 – your revised Intention

Put together the information that you have gathered in the previous two steps, and you may now wish to revise your Intention. This is often the case. Whereas the initial Intention tends to be woolly and vague, your revised Intention should be more focused. If so, write it as clearly as you can.

Remember that the Intention is defined as a goal whereby the business meets the needs of its customers within the context of the marketplace.

As an example, a nursing home developed an Intention that was 'to keep the quality and environment of the home at such a high level, that potential relatives and patients can feel this in the first seven minutes of entering the home . . . and beyond'.

This came from realising that the first impression meant everything in the placing of a patient.

Having established the Intention, you are ready for the next step. You have a message that will act as a guide to you, both this week and in the near future. Asking which option is likely to lead you closer to your Intention is an important factor in the decision-making process.

While your Intention must remain as flexible as the environment around the business, it is unlikely that further amendment will be needed this week.

Issue identification

It is now necessary to cover the last part of the Information Gathering stage and uncover what the key issues are in the business. Then, when you finally go to your staff and ask them for their input, you will know exactly where you need to direct their attention. By the end of today you should also have identified some ideas to get started with.

If necessary you can do this on your own, but to get the best results you will want to involve as many people as possible. This will certainly include members of the management team, but also staff and customers.

There is a seven-step method for collecting this information. The first three are quite general:

1 Look for clues in your financial accounts.
2 Generally observe what is going on in the business at the moment.
3 Get as many people in the business as possible to complete a general survey.

After reviewing this information, the next four will be more
focused and will be influenced by the results from the initial
review:

4 Interview some of the staff in more detail.
5 Telephone some of your customers or collect them
   together in a focus group.
6 Observe areas where particular issues have been raised.
7 Map out the processes and systems that are causing
   concern.

There may be no need to cover all of these last four. At the
end, all the information needs to be collected and
rationalised, so that it can be prioritised. This makes it
important to keep detailed notes whatever you are doing.

Step 1 – financial accounts

Your financial accounts will give you some initial clues as to
places to look. Consider the trend of the results over the last
few months or years. Probably the most important ratio is
that of Return on Equity (for companies) or Return on Capital
(for unincorporated bodies). These are the ratios of
profitability to owners' funds in the business. As a minimum,
this ought to exceed the best savings rate that you can get
with a bank. Given the risk involved in investing in a
business the return should be a lot higher.

If you need to look in more detail, the Return on Funds ratio
can be broken down into three areas:

- The ratio of profit after all costs to sales – the margin
- The ratio of sales to total assets – productivity
- The ratio of assets to owners' funds – leverage

If any of these trends is downwards then you should drill down into more detail. If the margin is falling, is it the costs that vary with each sale that are rising (variable costs) or the fixed costs that are there irrespective of whether a sale is made? If the productivity ratio is falling, is this because sales are falling or because stock or debtors are increasing?

Of even more use would be to compare your results against those of competitors in a benchmarking exercise. There are various agencies that can provide this type of information, including trade associations.

This information will not, however, give you the whole story. The problem with your accounts is they give you the results of what has happened, but they are the result of a great many individual actions. To get closer to the whole story you will need to involve other people.

Step 2 – general observation

First impressions count for a lot in business and in life. If you have a place of business where staff work or customers visit then clues can be found just by trying to look through their eyes at what they see each time they enter. This is easier said than done if you have been there for some time.

Start outside the building and put yourself in the shoes of a prospective customer or employee. The first thing to do is to rate the 'initial impressions'. On a scale from 1 (poor) to 7 (excellent), give ratings to:

- The general appearance of the buildings from the outside
- The standard of welcome both outside and inside
- The neatness of reception
- The standard of customer care that is displayed

If you have a factory or production and storage area, use the same scale to rate:

- The general appearance of the production area and its layout
- The organisation of stock and any work in progress
- The diligence of workers
- The interaction and co-operation between workers
- The age and use of equipment
- The evidence of work supervision

If you have offices, use the same scale to rate:

- The general appearance of the offices and its layout
- The adequacy and tidiness of storage space
- The diligence of staff
- The standard of office equipment

Finally think about any comments made by people who have recently visited for the first time. Were they complimentary and, if not, why might that be?

Step 3 – staff survey

This should be scheduled to happen early in the day. You can choose to present the survey to everyone in the business or select a sample. Covering everyone is normally the better option. It means that everyone gets an opportunity to add to the identification process and have his or her say. Sometimes, however, this is not possible. You may not be able to get everyone together at the same time.

If you are choosing a sample, it needs to be as representative as possible. You can do this by grade, by division or by activity (sales/production etc.). Key management should certainly be included, as should the people who know most about what is going on in the business. These must include staff who have customer contact, especially the receptionist!

As far as the design of the survey is concerned, it needs to be as simple as possible, asking questions in a general way that most people will have an answer for. The following survey (on pages 42–4) is divided into a number of sections so that you can gain a picture of the organisation. The model for the survey is the 'Business Triangle', which suggests that for an organisation to be successful it needs to be strong in three key areas:

- Management
- Products and Services
- Finance

Example staff survey

Part One – Management

The vision	1–7 or n/a
We have a written Business Plan which has been updated in the past year	
Management and staff are clear about the future direction of the business	
There is no resistance to change in the organisation	
Performance is measured regularly and feedback is given	
Staff are encouraged to ask questions and give opinions to management	

The people	1–7 or n/a
We offer flexible contracts to suit the organisation	
Staff are appropriately trained	
The disruption caused by absence is minimal	
Pay is related to performance	
Staff are asked for good ideas and are rewarded for them	

The systems	1–7 or n/a
The business makes proper use of systems to reduce time and effort	
We set and monitor budgets	
The key ratios of the business are tracked	
Staff are kept informed of matters that affect them	
We comply with all Regulations that are relevant to us	

Example staff survey (*continued*)

Part Two – Products and services

The selling process	1–7 or n/a
Everyone is involved with the marketing of the business	
We look after existing profitable customers and clients	
We are profit driven and not sales motivated	
We monitor enquiries and conversion rates	
We actively seek feedback from customers and clients	

The buying process	1–7 or n/a
Our regular suppliers help us to reduce costs	
Purchasing needs are planned ahead	
Major costs are put out to tender regularly	
We reduce the size of orders unless there is a bulk discount	
The quality and accuracy of goods received are always checked	

The production process	1–7 or n/a
All work is planned to be completed quickly and effectively	
We have removed any part of the process where no value is added	
Work moves through the operation with no delay	
Storage space is utilised effectively/files are easily retrieved	
Delivery routes are planned and efficient	

Example staff survey (*continued*)

Part Three – Finance

Operating assets	1–7 or n/a
There is no wasted room in our buildings	
We have no obsolete stock or work in progress	
Invoicing takes place as soon as possible after the sale	
Debt collection practices are applied rigorously	
Supplier invoices are paid when they are due	

Overheads and taxation	1–7 or n/a
Staff are encouraged to find ways of reducing overheads	
Travel and entertainment costs are tightly controlled	
Our insurance broker gets the best deal for us	
We have a tax planning session before the end of the financial year	
The tax bill is minimised by efficiently extracting profits	

Cash and funding	1–7 or n/a
Rolling cash flow forecasts are prepared	
We are honest about funding problems that arise	
The structure of funding matches the assets	
Keyman insurance is in place to protect the value of the business	
We monitor bank balances regularly	

The questions are designed to be general ones that will apply to just about every organisation, but feel free to change them to statements that are more relevant to your organisation. Each statement should be scored between 7 (where there is full agreement that the statement applies to the business) and 1 (where there is total disagreement that the statement applies to the business). There will be some statements for which people will not have sufficient knowledge to have an opinion. These should be left blank.

It is essential that everyone knows that the replies to this survey will be confidential and that none of the scores will be attributed. If you suspect that this may be a problem and that people will not give their honest opinions, then bring in someone independent to process the returned forms for you.

Present the survey to your team as early as possible in the day. Ideally you should get them all together, or do this in groups if there are too many. To get the best response you will need to explain:

- Why the survey is being done and where it fits into the Profit Improvement week
- The incentives that you agreed on Monday for everyone who takes part
- That the replies will be confidential and no scores will be attributed to individuals
- That they can therefore be as honest as possible
- That they should focus on the whole organisation rather than their individual department or division
- That they should complete the survey and return it immediately

If it is not possible to get everyone together, you can send it to everyone, but with the key points in the message.

Getting the surveys back as soon as possible means that the results of the three parts of the survey can then be averaged, excluding 'not applicable' scores. By running the scores for each section through a 'Radar' chart, you will be able to analyse your organisation in the three key areas against the perfect 7 score. It should look something like this:

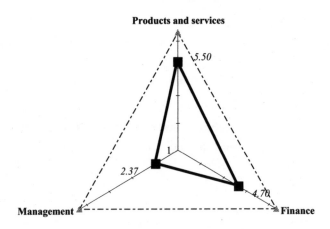

Example business triangle

In this example it can be seen that the management part is the weakest. In fact, if this organisation gets much weaker in that area then the triangle could be ready to fall over. Wherever the weakest areas are, identify the statements that have caused this. You will need to look beyond the simple averages. For example, any statement where 50 per cent or more of the respondents scored 3 or less is also an area of weakness. Any statement where more than 30 per cent score 2 or less is clearly an area of concern. These are clues as to the problems that could be holding back the profitability of the business.

At the end of this section you should have a list of general issues that have been collected together from the work to date. It is unlikely, however, that you will know the full reasons behind them. These areas now need to be looked at in more detail through the following techniques.

Step 4 – staff interviews

The results of the survey will give you more information than just looking at the accounts, but you will need to dig deeper to get the best from the exercise. Interviewing just a few of the staff, and asking the right questions, will produce a flood of useful information.

As the staff answered the survey anonymously, you will have to select those to be interviewed in more detail based on your knowledge of them. Who are the more positive members of the team? Who are the ones who have had good ideas in the past?

Invite them individually into a quiet room and start by re-emphasizing the purpose of the week and the importance of their honesty. Ask some of these general questions:

- What is your understanding of the direction that the organisation is heading in?
- How could customer satisfaction be improved?
- What upsets the customers so much that they consider leaving?
- How is staff morale and how do you think it could be improved?
- Where are staff most stretched?
- What is the one thing that has brought you closest to leaving?
- Is everyone adequately trained? Where is the greatest need?
- Where are the bottlenecks in our processes?
- How could the quality of work be improved?
- If you were in charge, what three changes would you make?

After these general questions have been answered, you will then be able to see if they can explain what is behind some of the other general issues that have arisen so far. You should allow an hour for each interview and none should last more than 90 minutes. This will give you enough time to find out what you need to, but not too much that the session drags on.

The interviews should ideally be either side of lunch. You will need the break to absorb the issues that arise in the morning.

Step 5 – customer interviews or focus groups

It would also be helpful to interview maybe four of your key customers over the phone. These calls should take no more than 20 minutes each. Alternatively, arrange for a number of them to visit and form a focus group.

Explain the purpose of the call or the meeting and encourage them to be as honest as possible. They should be pleased to help you if it means that you are trying to improve customer service! If you are meeting them, this would be a good opportunity to treat them to a meal afterwards as a 'thank you'.

The following general questions will warm things up:

- How easy is it to do business with us?
- What would improve the business relationship?
- Why do you choose to do business with us rather than the competition?
- How would you rate the sales people that you work with?
- How would you rate the operations people that you deal with?
- What percentage of the time do we get it right first time?
- How responsive are we to fixing problems?
- How is our administration?
- What would cause you to do more business with us?

Should any issues arise from a question, dig further to get to the real issues and then raise general issues that you have discovered which impact on the customer.

Step 6 – observe specific areas

If there was a specific area of the business that was identified as being a problem area, a better alternative to interviewing the staff who work there is to go to that area. A combination of watching what is happening and asking questions of the staff as work is carrying on should uncover the reasons for the problems that have been identified.

Step 7 – review systems and processes

If a problem cannot be pinned down to one part of a business, it may be necessary to map out an entire system or process to spot the cause of the problem and identify the reasons.

Take the example of a factory that manufactures widgets. These go through a number of processes from raw material to finished product. Along the way, the parts need to be transported from one operation to another and inspected. Inevitably there can be some delay along the way. However, the business boasts that it holds stocks that average only four days of raw materials and two days of finished goods. It has been found that the procedure is as follows:

- The raw materials are taken from the store 32 hours after it was delivered. It takes 15 minutes for the storekeeper to select the materials and 20 minutes to take these parts to the start of the production line.
- The first parts are assembled in 70 minutes; there is then a five-minute journey to the next part of the line.
- There is a hold-up of eight minutes before fitting takes place and fitting takes 25 minutes.

- There is a three-minute journey to the testing area where the queue is normally six hours.
- It takes one minute to test the widget before going to finished stock.

Example process map

No	Step Description	Time (mins)	Operation	Transport	Inspect	Store	Delay
1	Raw material (waiting in stores)	1920				✓	
2	Parts select	15			✓		
3	Transport to line	20		✓			
4	Assembly	70	✓				
5	Transport	5		✓			
6	Hold up	8					✓
7	Fitting	25	✓				
8	Transport to testing	3		✓			
9	Queue	360					✓
10	Testing	1			✓		
11	Finished stock	960				✓	
	Total	3387					
	Operations	95					
	Percentage Operations	2.8%					

When the process is looked at in this way, it becomes easier to see how and where changes need to be made. During anything other than an 'operation', no value is being added and 'waste' of some description is taking place.

Collect and rationalise the information
Your notes may now be quite confusing, with lots of information covered. In order to bring some order to your notes, it is wise to go through each point individually, and transfer them into a more logical order.

Mindmap: One alternative is to use a number of Mindmap diagrams, which will give a visual view of the issues. This involves taking a separate piece of paper for each of the nine sections of the Business Triangle, e.g. The Vision, The People etc. Put these headings in the centre of each page and transfer your main issues onto the page that most closely fits. These will be connected as branches to the main heading. Other issues may then become smaller branches.

Affinity diagram: Otherwise, write all the points that you find on a stack of sticky notes and then arrange them into related groups. After you have grouped the notes, develop a title or heading. The heading should be short and describe the main theme of the group that it represents. Now look for relationships between them that may mean that groups need to be combined.

Find and prioritise the key issues
Review each point that you have come up with, no matter how small. Some of the points will have clustered with others to become more significant.

Bear in mind the *7 Golden Questions of Profit Improvement*:

1 Where could staff become more involved in the planning and running of the business?
2 How can more of the better customers be retained?
3 How can you sell more to existing customers?
4 Where are the opportunities to sell to more customers?
5 Where is the waste in the process?
6 How could the organisation's systems be improved?
7 Where is the conflict between departments?

There should be two main areas that you have identified:

- Issues where solutions have presented themselves during the day, which are worthy of further consideration
- Issues that are clearly important and holding the organisation back, but which have not yet been resolved

The solutions that are worthy of further consideration will be considered first thing tomorrow. You should exclude, however, anything that could not be solved in a group context, or which is personal. These need to be solved separately. Ideally you should be left with no more than seven unresolved issues. Should you have more than this number, some further rationalisation will be necessary. Some of them will have to be targeted at a later date. Which are the ones that you believe to be most urgent in needing to be rectified? In particular, which ones are holding the organisation back from reaching the destination identified yesterday?

When you are down to no more than seven issues, gather together the details of all of them. A useful structure to use is the 'I-Scan', which is summarised on the next page. This is an information gathering tool, but it can sometimes help problems to dissolve without any further effort. Some of the 12 sections may not be relevant.

Sorting the issues

With the fuller understanding of what each issue represents, are any of them connected? Having established the connections between issues, what comes first and could be causing the other? After putting these all together in a diagram, it can often be found that just one or two key issues are at the root of many others. These need to be identified and confronted tomorrow, not avoided.

Conclusion

At the end of this day, collect together the results of the accounts review and survey, the ideas and solutions that you want to consider further on Friday morning and the details of the issues that you want to be resolved as soon as possible.

The Information Gathering part of the exercise is now complete.

Martin Leith's I-scan

Indications
What are the signs that action is required? A key question is this: If, while you were sleeping tonight, a miracle were to occur and the problem were to clear up instantly, how would you know when you woke up that the miracle had happened?

Influences
What are the contributing factors and antecedents?

Implications
What are the likely consequences? What benefits are gained as a by-product of the problem remaining unsolved?

Interests
Who has an interest in things changing? Who has an interest in things staying the same? Who will be affected to a greater or lesser extent by the change? Who is the owner of the problem or the initiator of the change programme? Who else is involved?

Impulses
What might help the innovation or change process?

Impediments
What might impede, inhibit or hinder the innovation or change process?

Inter-related issues
How does the issue under consideration connect with other issues? What is the problem costing? Consider actual cost and opportunity cost, past and future. Also consider non-monetary costs: time, emotional energy, etc.

Inconsistencies
What are the exceptions to the problem pattern? What conditions are present when the problem does not happen?

Inefficacies
What has been tried that has not worked? What do these attempts have in common? Is there a pattern?

Injunctions
What are the givens, the positive and negative specifications, the parameters, the musts and must nots? What is non-negotiable?

Intuitions
Do you have any hunches or gut feelings about this project?

Inventory
What resources and capabilities do you have at your disposal? What resources and capabilities are missing?
- Time
- People
- Support
- Information
- Accommodation
- Money
- Skills
- Specialist knowledge
- Equipment
- Other resources (specify)

Idea generation

You may have thought that going through the Information Gathering stages alone would have been sufficient to generate plenty of ideas. While you will have uncovered some ideas yesterday, experience suggests that these are merely scratching the surface of what is possible.

To date you are likely to have collected only the more obvious ideas that are unlikely to address the key issues that the business faces. Having decided what the key issues are at the present time, there is a need to have a special event to tackle them. Getting your key staff together to focus on these key issues will be the object of the day.

Planning the day

For a start the day needs a title. Calling it a 'Profit Improvement Day' does not work for everyone – 'Improvement Day' is perhaps better. The choice is up to you – what will work best in your business?

The next thing to decide is who from the business should be involved in the day. It was said earlier that the secret of successful Profit Improvement is to use *everyone's* ideas and abilities to the greatest advantage.

People who you interviewed yesterday should certainly be there. They will probably have had some additional thoughts since the interview and be willing to share them. In addition look for people who are:

- Informed – the people who know what is going on in the business
- Integral – the key individuals in the business
- Interested – only people who want to be there should attend
- Incisive – people who get straight to the point
- Inquiring – people who ask questions
- Inventive – the creative people who will have some solutions
- Impatient – these people will push for action today and keep things moving tomorrow

When considering how many people to involve, remember that out of every seven to ten people, one of them needs to be happy to be a group leader.

The agenda of the day should be split into seven sessions:

1 Introduction to the day (10 minutes)
2 Intentions of the business (15 minutes)
3 Information gathering results (30 minutes) followed by a break
4 Ideas workshop session
5 Interval for lunch
6 Issues workshop session
7 Ideas plan review from the different groups (20 minutes)

From this, it can be seen that the day starts 'global', before going 'local' and reverting back to 'global' again.

The invitation to the day should explain what is planned in detail. A copy of the agenda should therefore be attached along with a list of the key issues that the organisation faces.

Staff need to be aware that they will be asked to identify the seven 'I's' of the solution and therefore:

- Consider the issues that the business is facing and **Identify** a wide range of **Ideas**
- Gain consensus as a group and decide whether these ideas should be **Implemented**
- Agree the **Individual** responsible for implementing the idea, its **Impact** on the business, **Input** required and the **Increase** in profits that would result from successful implementation.

By giving them notice of these things prior to the session, staff have a chance to think about the possible solutions.

The venue for the workshop should, if possible, be away from the business. This is desirable as it reduces the chance that anyone will be disturbed during the day and makes it easier for people to focus on what can possibly be achieved rather than feeling restricted.

When selecting and setting a meeting room:

- Look for one with little or no outside noise and as much natural light as possible
- Tables and chairs need to be arranged in a horse-shoe shape with space in between
- Allow tea, coffee, soft drinks and fruit to be available all the time

At a more detailed level:

- You may need to borrow or hire a computer projector and screen to present the results of the survey and the final plan
- There needs to be a flipchart and pens for each group
- Each attendee should be provided with paper and pens for notes
- There should be place cards for each person, particularly where some of the delegates are not well known to each other
- Make sure you have plenty of your chosen incentives, e.g. the cash or vouchers, ready (three or four for each person should be allowed for)
- Each group leader needs a number of copies of the blank Ideas Plan to record the ideas (an example will be presented later)

On the day itself

You and the other organisers will need to arrive early to ensure that all the arrangements have been made correctly and to be available to welcome attendees as they arrive. It is helpful if a pack is presented to each attendee on arrival that includes:

- The workshop objectives
- The agenda
- A summary of the key issues identified

- The groups and their leaders, if there are more than ten attendees
- The rules of the workshop sessions
- A 'Seven Ideas to Improve Performance and Profitability' form (see page 67)
- Implementation worksheets

The groups should be mixed. It is preferable if the people have not worked together before.

The three initial presentations in the agenda are essential in order to set the scene and warm people up, but they should not overrun.

Session 1 – introduction
The short introduction should explain the structure and objectives of the day. It should cover a summary of the process that is being worked through this week. The position and importance of the day in the week should be explained.

Session 2 – intentions of the business
The presentation by the owner or Chief Executive should explain the Intention of the business that was decided on Tuesday, as this will give a focus to the proceedings. The emphasis should be on honesty and candour, demonstrating that the business has faced reality. If there is time, allow people to comment.

Session 3 – Information Gathering
The presentation continues the scene setting and should cover:

- The highs and lows of the staff survey
- A radar diagram showing the Business Triangle
- A summary of the ideas that came from the survey and interviews that you believe should be implemented
- A list of the key issues that remain

The presentation might also cover a summary of the trading position of the organisation, unless this is common knowledge. Many of the delegates are unlikely to have much idea about the financial stability of the organisation. It can only help to put things in perspective. A couple of slides that show the profit and loss account and balance sheet, with an explanation of what the numbers mean, can be very useful in helping people to understand how the business is doing and how it may need their help. The more information that can be given, the better it is. Go back to the work that you did at the start of yesterday when looking at the financial accounts of the business. Is there information here that could be shown to everyone?

If you were able to get any information on competitors it would be useful to show some of this as well, identifying where they seem to be ahead of you.

Session 4 – ideas workshop
The two sessions either side of the lunch interval will form the main part of the day. What has gone before has been important preparation and before the delegates break up into their groups one final piece of preparation is needed. Everyone should be asked the question:

'If we are successful in identifying additional profits today, how would you like to see it used?'

The answers that generally come back are varied but are likely to include things like:

- Higher pay, benefits or dividends
- Investment in new equipment or marketing and sales effort
- Reduction of debt
- The ability to recruit specialist staff
- Buying other businesses

At this particular point in the process, the question is key. Allowing as many people to have their say at this point means that everyone should see that there is something in the results for them.

It was said earlier that there needs to be a leader or facilitator for each group of ten delegates. The most important thing that the facilitators have to bear in mind is that their role is not to deliver ideas and solutions, but to serve their group. After introducing themselves and making sure that everyone knows each other, the first job of the facilitator is to lay out the ground rules. This is best done by explaining the WORKSHOP RULES which are in two parts. The first part explains what delegates are to do and the second covers the objectives of the facilitator.

The delegates will:

Work together as a team – *the results will always be better than if you all work as individuals.*

One person to talk at a time – *if more than one person is talking, then someone is not listening.*

Respect each other's opinions – *it is dangerous to scoff at other people.*

Keep an open mind about everything – *closed minds can lead to a closed business.*

Speak up and say what needs to be said – withhold nothing – *it is only by speaking up that the best ideas get heard.*

Help the group to use its time effectively – be concise – *time will be short and will fly during the sessions.*

Only discuss key issues – avoid side-tracks and tangents – *with limited time available, people need to keep to the point.*

Personal attacks and sarcasm are unhelpful – *they are banned.*

The facilitators will:

Record the key decisions taken – *by writing down the actions and calling them back, everyone will be clear about what has been agreed.*

Unleash the power of the group – *encourage them to work together.*

Let the discussion flow, but keep focused on the key issues.

Encourage everyone to have his or her say – *sometimes the quietest people have the best thoughts to offer.*

Serve the group in a neutral capacity and call foul if rules are broken – *you can call foul by rustling paper.*

WORKSHOP RULES

It can be seen that the skilful facilitator will be able to:

- Be a neutral servant to the group and focus its energy
- Be more concerned about the process of the session than the content
- Help the group to make the greatest progress by abiding by the rules
- Swiftly move items not on the agenda or not agreed onto another meeting

The skilful facilitator will also be able to 'read' the group by watching the body language and reactions of individuals. They need to be attentive to whoever is speaking at the time while watching for others who may want to contribute. The skilful facilitator will also be able to manage their own body language by, for example:

- Using a voice that encourages participation
- Knowing when to pause and use silence
- Standing or sitting back from the table if more authority is required

These are particularly important at the start of any session, especially in a group that has not worked together before and needs to get used to one another before they discuss the key issues. For this reason, the first session should start with some form of open discussion to get things moving in the right direction.

Either ask everyone, 'How would you like to see the organisation in seven years?', or alternatively consider using some of the following:

- What makes this organisation successful?
- What are our (a) strengths and (b) weaknesses?
- What are the (a) opportunities and (b) threats that we face?
- If you could change one thing in the organisation, what would it be?

Especially in the opening period, the facilitator should ask open questions, such as: 'What do think about . . .?'; 'What is your opinion . . .?'; 'If Mark thinks that we should . . . then what do you think?' Closed questions should only be used when the facilitator is trying to close and end a discussion of a particular point. For example, 'Do you agree that . . .?' Comments and questions should be re-directed between individuals to give others the opportunity to voice their opinion, and if a comment needs to be clarified then the facilitator can paraphrase for understanding and clarity.

The 'Five Whys' technique can be useful in getting down to the bones of a problem. Using this, the question to each answer given is 'Why?' However, watch for defensive responses.

Even at this early stage it will be clear that there are a number of 'difficult participants', who for various reasons are ignoring the rules. The most common ones are:

- *Talkative Tim/Tina* – he or she may be well informed, but could be eager to show off knowledge. A reminder of the need to be concise could be along the lines of, 'That is interesting – what do others think?'

- *Arguing Alan/Alice* – they may have a combative personality or be upset by an individual point. Either find something that they say that you can genuinely agree with and move on to something else, or toss an obviously incorrect remark that they make to the group. As a last resort take them to one side during the next break.

- *Rambling Rob/Rose* – easily strays from the issue being discussed and cannot find a way back, so carries on! When they pause for breath, thank them, restate the relevant key issues and say, 'We really need to get back to the subject' before moving on.

- *Silent Simon/Simone* – they are probably shy by nature or lacking in confidence. Rather than asking them directly, ask the opinion of the person next to them and then move on to them. These people tend to be listening and tend to have something important to say if given the opportunity.

When the facilitator thinks that the group is warmed up and that everyone has contributed to the discussion, he or she can turn the group's attention to the 'Seven Ideas to Improve Performance and Profitability' form, which should have seven boxes on one page that look like this:

Idea: Initials:

Issue that this idea will solve:

Everyone should complete just the first box with their best idea and fill in their initials, then pass the form to their left. Having received a new form, the second idea can be one that they already had in mind, or another idea that could have been inspired by what their neighbour wrote. If someone gets stuck, they pass the form on and wait to receive the next one from their right. Seeing what others have written is often inspiring. The process continues until as many boxes as

possible have been completed. It is generally found that the last few ideas, while being the most difficult to get out, may be the best!

The next step is to collect the ideas and take an inventory. If you have ten people in a group and each paper has seven ideas, there could be up to 70 ideas to consider. Therefore the ideas need to be broken down into groups and it has been found that doing this by ease of implementation works well.

This means that you now need three pieces of flipchart paper for each group. These can be headed:

- Indisputably easy
- In-betweens
- Immensely difficult

Having returned the sheets to whoever wrote the first idea on it, start by asking everyone for the idea on his or her sheet that would be the easiest to implement. This will be the one which, if agreed, could even be put into practice tomorrow. Your description on the 'Indisputably easy' flipchart should take up no more than one line. Include the initials of the person whose idea it was. People may say things in this section that the facilitator thinks will be far from easy and extremely complicated, but the temptation to say this must be resisted. If anything, try to greet each idea with a positive comment such as, 'Yes, we might try that' or, 'That's an interesting thought, we should look at that at some point.' Also to be resisted is any detailed discussion at this stage. If the idea has real merit then there will be time for consideration later.

The second stage is to ask everyone for the idea on their sheet that would be the hardest to implement and record these in the same way on the 'Immensely difficult' flipchart. That will leave you to collect ideas that people have left that have not been covered already. These can either go on the 'In-between' sheet or the person can nominate one of the other flipcharts to put them on.

After everyone is happy that the ideas that they would like to have discussed are somewhere on the flipcharts, go to the 'Indisputably easy' chart and let the group choose the one that they would like to discuss in detail first.

With the group having agreed the easiest one to start with, the person whose idea it was in the first place should explain it in some more detail to the group. The facilitator should then let the discussion flow, with the WORKSHOP RULES in the background, being used only when necessary.

Each idea should be discussed in three steps, with people giving their opinions of why the idea is (1) Ingenious, and (2) Inadequate, before agreeing how it can be (3) Improved. Be aware that no matter how simple and straightforward the idea may seem, this first idea is usually the most difficult to get agreed. Everyone needs to have his or her say, no matter how brief. When you believe that everyone has reached a consensus, ask for the idea to be captured, using the example on the following page as a model.

- *Idea description* should describe the initiative that is going to make the business more profitable. This should be done in bullet point form to capture the essence of the idea rather than the detail.

SAMPLE IDEAS PLAN

Idea no	Idea description	Idea contributor	Impact 1=high 5=low	Input required 1=low 5=high	Implemen-tation date	Individual responsible	Inrease in profits	Comments
1								
2								
3								

Adapted from *All About Earnings* by Barry R. Schimel and Gary Kravitz

- *Idea contributor* is the person who wrote the idea on the list. This person should be rewarded with one of your chosen incentives at this point. The first time that this happens often has a remarkable effect on the group.

- *Impact* on the business should be graded on a scale of 1 to 5, with a '1' being given to a high impact while '5' is given to one of low importance.

- *Input required* should also be graded between 1 and 5, with a '1' being given where there is little input required while '5' is given to the most difficult ones.

- *Implementation date* is the date when it is planned that the idea will be put into practice and earning additional revenues or profit.

- *Individual responsible* is the one person from the group who volunteers to take the idea on when the day is ended and make sure that it gets implemented. It does not have to be the most senior person in the group who takes this on. Often the person whose idea it was in the first place will feel strongly enough about it to make sure that the idea does not go to waste. This person should also be rewarded with one of the incentives. No matter how straightforward the idea may seem, implementation is rarely easy!

- *Increase in profits* is often the final test for an idea. If the group cannot demonstrate through some simple assumptions that the idea is going to improve performance and profitability, then should time be taken up with implementing it? If this proves difficult, then serious consideration should be given to leaving the idea to one side and moving on to something else.

People can get carried away with the positive emotions of the session and have wildly inflated views of the impact of the ideas. The facilitator's job is always to test the assumptions and if there is any doubt as to the prudence of the estimates, they should offer to halve or even quarter the assumptions. Unrealistically high targets are as demotivating as low or non-existent targets.

When each idea has been captured in this form, the facilitator needs to make it clear that the discussion on the subject is closed and it is time to move on to another idea. This can be done by clearly crossing it from the flipchart and rewarding the 'Idea contributor' and 'Individual responsible'. Each time, he or she should allow the group to decide which of the remaining ideas is to be discussed next. The first two or three ideas should come from the 'Indisputably easy' list.

When the facilitator is satisfied that the process is running smoothly, then the other two flipcharts can be opened up for consideration.

If other ideas come up which are in a related area, take care not to get diverted. These ideas should be captured in an 'Ideas Bin' for consideration later.

Before the interval for lunch, it is useful to summarise the ideas that have been captured during the session. Delegates should be asked to consider the remaining ideas and think about those that they really want to cover at some point in the next session. Ask for their feedback on the morning session.

Session 5 – interval for lunch workshop
During the interval, where there have been a number of
groups at work, the group leaders should:

- Spend some time together to discuss how they
  found the 'Ideas workshop' session and reveal what
  has been agreed. It is surprisingly rare that two
  groups will have been discussing exactly the same
  idea, but sometimes they will have attempted a
  solution to the same problem from different but
  complementary directions.
- Discuss which issues definitely need to be covered
  in the next session, especially those key issues that
  were identified yesterday as driving many others. No
  two groups should talk through the same solutions
  this afternoon.
- Be available to take comments from team members
  that they might not have wanted aired in the session.
- If possible, record the plans to date on one
  combined set.

Session 6 – issues workshop
The afternoon session will have a slightly different format.
Groups are now given a short-list of the issues that have not
been addressed already and are able to choose one only.

Each group discusses its particular issue. The first approach
is known as 'Imagineering'. The group is asked to describe a
time in the future when the issue has been solved and there
are no problems of any kind. From this description they are
asked to work backwards and describe the steps that were
necessary to achieve this. When this has gone as far as it can,

they can then work forwards 'Incrementally' from where they are now and describe each step that needs to be taken. This will not necessarily lead to the same place that they started from. Should this process falter, encourage some way out or odd ideas. Think of the 'impossible' and ask, 'Wouldn't it be wonderful if . . . ?'

Even though the issues being discussed are likely to be harder than those covered in the morning, the afternoon session is often easier and flows better as the clock ticks on.

Before breaking again, summarise the extra progress made to the group and clear any final issues that may be there.

Session 7 – Ideas Plans review
After the break, get all the groups back together. Each facilitator should present the ideas from their group to everyone. If these can be displayed on a screen for everyone to see that would be an advantage. This will explain in outline the ideas agreed to be taken forward. Remember to include the ideas that came out from yesterday's survey and interviews.

The conclusion session
During this concluding session, thank everyone for their contribution during the day and explain the next steps. In outline the next steps will be that:

- Early tomorrow all of the ideas are to be considered and prioritised by a small team
- an overall plan will be produced that will be circulated to everyone and a number of people will be contacted to agree how these high priority ideas are to be progressed as soon as possible

It is worth explaining to everyone at this point that it is most unlikely that all of the ideas will be able to go ahead straight away. To do this risks the organisation suffering from 'Initiative overload' and important operational work being left.

The final task is to ask everyone to complete the following sentence:

'I intend to support this Improvement Process by . . .'

Get as many people as possible to read out what they have written. This reinforces their commitment to follow through later.

When the day is over

Now you can turn your attention to those issues that could not be raised today. Do any of the initiatives on the Ideas Plans to date address these? If not, what actions now need to be taken? This can sometimes be established by going through the stages of the process for each problem. Therefore write out for each one:

1 *Introduction* to the problem.
2 *Incentives* for solving the problem. Where is the pain to be avoided and where are the gains to be made?
3 *Intention:* where do you hope to get to?
4 *Issues:* what are they?
5 *Ideas:* list up to seven options, and then comment on them before choosing one or a combination.

Include your chosen solution on the Ideas Plan in the same format, although these may need to be ones that you yourself are responsible for.

But we can't afford to take a day to do this!

This is a familiar cry at the suggestion that the organisation takes a day away from the business. Many people believe that they are indispensable and are then amazed when the organisation functions quite well without them when they take a holiday or are sick. Sometimes, however, it really is not possible to take too many people away for an entire day. This does not mean that there is no chance of making something of the opportunity.

One solution is to break the full day down into a series of 2-hour sessions, with the following format:

- *Session one:* the general introductions and the collection of the inventory of ideas.

- *Session two:* start with the 'Indisputably easy' ones only. Have a full discussion and plan them.
- *Session three and subsequent sessions:* start by reviewing the progress of the implementation of the ideas agreed in the previous session, before carrying on with the inventory of ideas and eventually tackling the tough remaining issues.

The benefit of this particular approach is clear. As everyone knows when the next session is, and that implementation is the first item on the agenda, implementation is more likely to happen!

Implementing the plans

Great ideas are meaningless and worthless unless they are successfully implemented, and it is common for additional profits not to be realised because of a breakdown in the implementation process. Anyone who has played sports such as football, tennis or golf, will know that the power in a shot comes not from hitting the ball, but from the follow through. And so it is with Profit Improvement.

This is the final part of the Information Gathering, Idea Generation and Implementation Guidance cycle. While in previous days we have tried to make the first two stages as complete as possible so that the best ideas have been planned at this stage, it is the work from today that will really determine the success of the project. For various reasons businesses find that putting ideas into operation is never easy.

It should be clear why it was recommended that existing initiatives be rationalised on Sunday. If you have followed the process through, you will now have plenty of initiatives to add to the list!

Why is implementation so difficult?

The answers to this question are many and varied. We have moved from the rational gathering and analysis of information and facts to implementation. This is now about people, and people are not fully rational. It is understood that as a race, humans are most comfortable when things stay the same. In fact we actively resist change wherever feasible.

Many of us enjoy studying a situation and analysing it. We then talk a lot about change and plan the necessary actions. Yet we do not always get beyond the talking stage. We stay in our comfort zone and avoid the hard work that change requires. In fact, when anything out of the ordinary happens, if anything 'changes', there starts an emotional roller coaster, whether we like it or not. This applies whether we are proposing to put a new sign over the photocopier telling people what to do when it goes wrong, to the introduction of a new computer system that will monitor the work that everyone is doing.

The journey has been described in many ways, one of which is the DREAD of change, which stands for:

- **Denial**
- **Resistance**
- **Exploration**
- **Acceptance**
- **Doing it**

The goal of implementation is to get all parties through the cycle as quickly and painlessly as possible.

Is there a solution?

Probably the biggest problem with implementation is that people think that having followed a process such as this, they should now be able to just take each idea, go ahead and implement or 'do it'. In fact, in all but the simplest example, this leads straight to difficulties and trouble. Pushing ahead too fast does not give enough time for those who are going through the DREAD cycle.

Think back to Sunday. You had the idea to improve profitability of the business. Could you just go ahead and 'do it'? We have seen that to be successful, there is a process that needs to be followed, in an order that was important. Here, on Friday morning, you are in a similar position. You have ideas that you want to do something with, but without a process to follow in a certain order, too much is left to chance. The following process has been designed to avoid such problems and the stages should be familiar to you as *they mirror the steps that have been taken to get this far!* This means that for each individual idea, there could be a need to:

- Make it clear what the incentives are
- Describe and review the Intention of the idea – what is it to achieve?
- Identify issues that will help or hinder implementation, and address the latter, such as questions of resources and skills
- Generate ideas to construct the detailed plan that is now required

If any of these is missing, success becomes less certain. Having followed this mini process for each idea it will be clear what needs to be done, and in what order.

Another major problem you may now face is rooted in the Law of Diminishing Intent. The further you get away from deciding to do something, the harder it becomes to get started. For this reason, key management of the organisation should get together to discuss the plans that came from the workshops early this morning. This might not be a popular meeting to call. People will have been away from the office yesterday and feel that they have a day's work to catch up on, but everything will lose momentum by not pressing ahead immediately.

The first thing to do is test the continuing validity of the ideas proposed. In the cold light of the new day, back in the real world of the business, each idea needs to be reconsidered in terms of:

- Does it bring the business closer to achieving its Intention?
- Is the idea still valid, having thought about it overnight?
- Is the value of its importance correct or does this need to be altered? Is the rating of input required correct, or does this need to be revised?
- Is the implementation date assigned to the idea realistic, or is it likely that more time will be needed to do this properly?
- Is the increase in profits realistic?
- Has the right individual been nominated to be responsible for the implementation of the idea?
- Most importantly, is there are good chance that the idea can be implemented?

In many cases it may be found that, even with the facilitator testing the assumptions during the workshop sessions, the groups have been too optimistic. While it could be considered dangerous to amend the plans in this way, doing so gives the week a greater chance of success than allowing unrealistic assumptions to be perpetuated and inappropriate individuals to continue their involvement.

Bear in mind the key issues that were identified at the start of Thursday. Solutions to the key issues that were identified to the workshop group ought to have the highest importance.

Having discussed each idea, it should be possible to produce a revised overall plan which has assumptions that management are now happy with. Some of the ideas may even have been taken out altogether, but it is better to do it at this stage than to use and waste valuable resources.

The list should now be prioritised. As the saying goes, 'To accomplish nothing, attempt everything'. To get an initial rough idea of the priorities, multiply the 'Impact' score of each idea with that of the 'Input required'. The lowest score will be 1 and the highest will be 25, although it will be rare to find any on the list that score that high. The most important ideas, which will take the smallest input to implement, should now be at the top of the list. Anything scoring more than 12 should be discounted immediately.

Starting at the top of the list with the lowest score, allocate a start date to each of the ideas, bearing in mind the resources in terms of time and costs that each idea will take up. The objective is to select some easy winners to get started with. These should be quick to implement rather than important to the organisation, as success in these can give momentum to the more difficult initiatives that are to follow. It may now be necessary to amend the implementation dates one final time. There should certainly be no more than ten initiatives to start now.

If necessary, have two lists. The first will have the top priority actions; the other will contain initiatives that will start next year. This year's plan should now be circulated to everyone who attended the workshop. This will need to be accompanied with some notes explaining why some ideas no longer feature in the plan and why the priorities might have changed. Finally, everyone should be told which ideas are being started first.

The 'Total Implementation Model' can now be started.

Step 1 – agree the incentives
Select the top idea and, bearing in mind the estimated profit increase, confirm the incentive linked to successful implementation. Remember that too many initiatives fail because there is no tangible benefit to the people who are managing the work.

Step 2 – confirm the Intention of the idea
Get together with the person who has taken responsibility for implementation. This person must now be involved in developing the practicalities. They may have some misgivings about having volunteered to take the task on, and will need to be coached if that is the case. You will be armed with a clear commitment from the top of the organisation to support the idea and give the appropriate staff the time to complete the project. If necessary, they will need to prioritise their existing duties and responsibilities.

In order to build the confidence of the individual responsible, help them to complete the following Intentions worksheet.

Keep in mind that although the goal may seem miles away, it gets closer only when you take this first step towards it.

INTENTIONS WORKSHEET
Initiative name:
Individual responsible:
Implementation completion date:
Intention description: a) the initiative goal   b) the issue solved   c) the increase in profits estimated
Initiative benefits:
Initiative deliverables:

Step 3 – identify the detailed issues
This second worksheet can now be completed:

ISSUES IDENTIFICATION WORKSHEET
Initiative name:
Individual responsible:
Implementation completion date:
Influences that might help the initiative, *e.g. a frustration with the way things are*:
Influences that might hinder the intitiative, *e.g. the impact on operations*:
Input that will be required, *e.g. time and cost*:
Individuals who will be able to help:
Important other factors to address:

Step 4 – generate the detailed ideas and plans

This third part of the worksheet can now be completed in draft. This sheet will be the one that needs to be most flexible. If at all possible collect together the individuals who need to be involved and who have volunteered to help. The same rules as applied yesterday continue to be useful:

IDEA AND PLAN WORKSHEET				
Initiative name:				
Individual responsible overall:				
Implementation completion date:				
Task number	Description of the task	Resources required	Due date	Individual responsible
010				
020				
030				
040				
050				
060				
070				
080				

Note that the task numbers do not start at 1, which means that tasks that are later identified can be slotted in, or sub-tasks can be inserted under each task.

This is quite a simple worksheet. For more complicated plans where there are a number of interdependencies, it would be recommended that project planning software be used. As with the overall Ideas Plan, this completed plan needs to be communicated. People need to know:

- What is happening?
- Where is it happening?
- Who will be affected?
- Why is it happening?
- How will it happen?
- When will it happen?

Step 5 – implementation!
The tasks can now be started before the Law of Diminishing Intent starts to kick in. For very simple ideas, following the Total Implementation Model might be overkill, but so long as little time is lost in completing the worksheets, this is one case where too much beats too little.

Step 6 – Select the next initiative and go back to step one!

There are no guarantees!

Even following the above system, there is only so much that anyone can do to be successful in implementing. To some extent, you cannot force staff to do something, even if they have signed up to it voluntarily. Incentives and sanctions may help. The best tool that you can ever have is the power of persuasion.

In the final analysis, 'It's all about implementation'. Without it, the most wonderful idea is of little value.

Inspection of progress

At the end of the week there remain just a few more important processes that need to be put in place. These involve constructing:

> - A plan for the follow-up of individual projects, to either reward progress or correct lack of progress
> - A system of measures that will enable you to monitor overall progress over the coming weeks and months

So the monitoring is tackled from two directions. Firstly, at the micro level, each of the initiatives that people are working on can be monitored to check that the plans are on track. At regular intervals these can be summarised and reported to management. Secondly, at the macro level, there are organisation level measures that will tell you how the overall project is going. The net profit as shown in financial accounts will be just one of these measures.

Tracking the individual projects

Some of the projects planned will have been taken on by people who have put projects into practice before. They will be happy to get on with the task and will report back to you at regular intervals. At the other extreme, some people will have done nothing like this before. They will need some serious support from you and others. They can be monitored as they are being helped through the process.

Soon after you start with this, it is an idea to split your overall list into three separate parts:

1 Projects completed in the last 12 months where the results are being monitored
2 Projects being worked on at the moment where results are being monitored
3 Projects that have not started yet which are at the planning stage

There are clear advantages to tracking the progress in a rigorous way:

- It becomes easier to spot those projects that are not progressing as fast as they should be, and be able to offer assistance
- Any resource issues can be addressed as soon as possible

For those who have not managed to complete their task – who present reasons and not results – engage them to find out what the real problems are and develop a solution. There will be some projects that, even after your analysis of them on Friday morning, will not achieve what was expected.

Do not be afraid to call a halt to initiatives that are not going anywhere, although where this happens there should be a full explanation to everyone concerned.

Measuring the success

At regular intervals, perhaps once a month, the progress
needs to be updated in the plan. How far through the project
are they now? This can probably be estimated as a percentage
of the total project. This time, the 'increase in profits' is based
on the actual increase achieved. This may be as difficult to
measure as the original estimate, but it is worth going
through those same assumptions.

As far as possible, the measures need to be easy to assimilate
and track. Visual presentation, for example in graphs, works
well.

- All current projects can be line-charted over time
  according to the percentage that they are complete
- Both completed and current projects can be charted
  to show their progress against the estimated profit
  increase in terms of value

Supporting the progress from the top

A review panel should be put together with the specific task
of monitoring the progress of the initiatives. With a senior
member of staff as the chairman, this should also include at
least one of the team leaders. This group should meet
regularly.

In addition, 'improvement progress update' should be an
agenda item on each management meeting agenda. Unless
the management visibly back the projects, then the interest
and motivation of the individuals responsible is likely to
wane.

Publishing the success

Positive feedback of results to staff is essential to keep the momentum. Any programme of this nature should have numerous successes. These must be made as visible and public as possible. You could have a special newsletter, articles in internal magazines, special meetings, as well as using noticeboards and memos. Word of mouth is rarely enough.

The news should be focused on:

- Easy wins achieved
- Milestones reached
- Projects fully implemented
- Results achieved

Success is part of the process and is important in ensuring continued confidence in the ongoing projects.

At least quarterly, if not monthly, these summaries should result in the rewards that were agreed on Monday being recognised.

Tracking the overall measures

At an organisation-wide level, your regular management accounts should be able to tell you whether the entire exercise is working. There are always other factors that will influence this other than your 'Profit Improvement in a Week' work, so unfortunately you are unlikely to get the credit for all improvements. It is usually found, however, that the impact of the process is felt wider than just the projects being worked on. Thursday's opportunity to get people together will often mean that they work better as a team afterwards.

The key ratios that you identified as part of the work on Wednesday can continue to be tracked to see how they improve. Results need to be well documented, accessible, quickly available and positively described. At least some of these measures should be non-financial in nature. There are often measures that provide an early indication of future improvements in net profit, such as customer satisfaction.

For example, customer focused ratios might include:

- Revenue per employee (net of returns)
- On time and in full order delivery
- Number of customers lost
- Number of customers gained
- Average customer age
- Value and quantity of returns/warranty claims
- Reputation in the marketplace
- Customer satisfaction scores

Employee satisfaction might be another area to monitor. If this is high or increasing then improvements in customer satisfaction and financial results usually follow. Intangibles such as this can be difficult to measure, but this can be done by creating 'opposite descriptions' for best case (scoring +7) and worse case (scoring –7) and asking employees their opinion.

There is no need to monitor everything. Use today to select the important measures to track and build up the history of them.

Congratulations! Everything is now in place. The only thing that is left for you to do is keep the momentum going over the coming weeks. This involves:

- Coaching all those who took responsibility for individual projects
- Monitoring the progress of projects completed and in progress
- Keeping the report on the agenda of management meetings
- Publicising and rewarding the success where projects have been completed

The secret now is consistency while the hard work continues to be carried out.

Final thoughts

You may be tempted, when going through this process in practice, to skip through stages to get some quicker results. To do so causes problems. For example, if you:

- Ignore the Introduction, then you will not be sure that the process is for you and your organisation
- Skip the Incentives, then you will face hard work later on and may never get started
- Avoid the Intentions, then you risk being confused, even heading off in the wrong direction and wasting time
- Miss the Issues, then you are unlikely to spot the real problems, which will continue to harm the organisation
- Ignore the Ideas, then everyone gets frustrated, especially if you know what the issues are
- Miss out on Implementation, then everyone has wasted a lot of time
- Allow the Inspection to lapse, then projects, especially the longer-term ones, will lose momentum

So each stage is important in the journey and missing or skipping through any one of them reduces the chances of success.

A summary of the week

These are the Seven Immutable Laws of Profit Improvement.

1 Improving profitability will be rewarding, but is not easy. Make sure that you are prepared to go all the way through the process before setting out.
2 This is a people process. It is people who will make the difference between success and failure. Make sure that they will be properly incentivised before you start and broadcast these plans.

3 Make sure that you are in the right business in the first place before you go trying to identify improvements to be made. The process may involve you in moving in a different business direction altogether.

4 Identify the key issues that are holding the business back. You can waste valuable time tackling trivial matters

5 Having identified the issues, your staff are likely to be the best people to be able to solve the problems. Get them together away from the business, achieve consensus on the solutions and capture the plans.

6 Never underestimate the difficulty of implementation. Go through the Total Implementation Model for each idea if necessary.

7 Above all else, remember that Profit Improvement is the result of implementing ideas in a structured way.